Anthology of Poems

Anthology of Poems

By
Dalward J DeBruzzi

E-BookTime, LLC
Montgomery, Alabama

Anthology of Poems

Copyright © 2009 by Dalward J DeBruzzi

All rights reserved. No part of this book may be reproduced or transmitted in any form or by any means, electronic or mechanical, including photocopying, recording, or by any information storage and retrieval system, without permission in writing from the copyright owner.

ISBN: 978-1-60862-123-1

First Edition
Published December 2009
E-BookTime, LLC
6598 Pumpkin Road
Montgomery, AL 36108
www.e-booktime.com

Contents

A Helping Hand Was Needed 7
Adjustments 11
Asian Symphony in America 13
Beginning to End 14
Devotion 15
Greatest Treasure of All 16
Henry Louis Gates Fails Badly 17
Is the Name Obama or Obuma? 21
Jackson Does it Again 23
Obama Health Care Plan 26
Ode to Self Proclaimed Mr. Clean –
    Governor Quinn 28
Parents 32
Persistence 34
Scorn Can Be Fatal 36
Seeking the One 38
Serving Who? 39
Thankfulness! 41
The Indian's Fate 42
Thinking Big 44
What I Say Sounds Good, You Can
    Quote Me Barack Obama 45
Why Illinois is 13 Billion in Debt 48
With Fondest Childhood Memories 51
Youth 53

A Helping Hand Was Needed

Fund raising abolitionists William, Lloyd Garrison and Harriet Beecher Stowe among thousands of others
Bought arms and financed the rebellion of John Brown who raised the conscience of all brothers

Brown lost his life and that of his son
To end a system and practice that all should shun

During Black history month you never hear about Brown. Why?
How quickly when you're not needed they let you down without a cry

Thousands of white underground railroad people risked life, prison, family and reputation
To assist people to a safe emancipation

These people who risked what is dear and near and maybe die
Are never mentioned in black lore it's clear, Why?

Abraham Lincoln issued a freedom paper
Promptly was assassinated for the Caper

His courage and leadership deserves accolades
Blacks never mention him, how memory fades. Why?

Anthology of Poems

Every president pushed hard with laws
Passing legislation with bite in its jaws

No president is mentioned during Black History inspection
Though they risked career and maybe an election. Why?

The abolitionists, presidents, and supporters too
Never are mentioned by blacks its true Why?

During black history month you never hear praise for these valiant souls
Is expressing appreciation out of blacks control?

In 140 years our amazing government propelled a black into the presidency we see
There is not recognition or thanks to be offered from blacks we agree. Why?

Fair play and justice would demand it be said clear and loud
White people aided, saved the blacks with head unbowed

IS THERE INGRATITUDE HERE?

Adjustments

Little Emile was sweet and good
Followed Mommie's advice and did what she should

In school teacher said she was smart
However Lacked sincerity and played a part

One day a doctor, then a singer even a nurse
These images inspired, excited, motivated no worse

College meant drama, theatrics fine arts
Sketches and roles and other parts

Auditioning and hoping, auditioning and hoping
Produced nothing but she managed coping

Staying fast, logical and remaining calm
Difficult, heart breaking, provided no balm

Back to school and adding a degree to her list
Gained accolades and success, she did persist

Life for Emilie today is successful and happy, contentment is great
Husband, children, practicing attorney, sublime happiness is her fate

Asian Symphony in America

Asians work hard, are steady and few
They commit the least crime of any group
Asians have lofty opinions of education it's true
Incarceration for them is not in their loop

Asians toil and strive without quotas or a set-aside
Achieving by doing, asking and demanding is not their thing
Everything they have gained is because they never cried
Active in medicine, the professions, they cling

By following the law in their existence each day
Generates respect, admiration, and general awe
The bards and poets would have much to say
That their manner would cause even a skeptic to jaw

Dalward J DeBruzzi

Beginning to End

Innocence and naiveté infants possess
Knowing little envelopes them in insulation

Teens charge with reckless abandon
Mind in recess

Maturity moves with sureness, caution and measured stride
Finality received eagerly and gently as a willing bride

A voice with definiteness orates I submit without sway
And gently, willingly, with repose fade away

Devotion

Help me search my heart my love
To see if there can be
Any hindrance from above
To keep thee from me

Help me to dispel the fear
When what I want is sharing
With a noble creature dear
With tenderness and caring

With luck, patience deep feelings
My earnest wish can appear
To engage my mystic queen in dealings
About matrimony and sublime cheer

Dalward J DeBruzzi

Greatest Treasure of All

Wee, sweet little angel of mine
Monumental blessing from a being divine

The joy, the happiness is total and complete
Little else of note or of value can compete

Innocence, beauty, purity, evokes thanks
Symbols of worth far exceeding contents of banks

Accumulations of rewards tally for future years
Ere a decent, admirable, upstanding adult appears

Guidance, sacrifice, shower of love, a fine creature emerges in detail
The cause, the motivator, inspirer caused the success to prevail

Henry Louis Gates Fails Badly

Henry came home late at night was
jimmying his front door, causing a
neighbor concern for him with fright

Police responded to burglary in progress
and investigated

When following procedure Gates insulted
the Policeman's mother with bother

Attempting to provoke a cop into hitting
him on the head

Gates was insulting, non cooperative,
enough said

To gain cheap publicity and create disharmony and be beguiling

Gates appealed to Obama and claimed profiling

All we have here is a law breaker in the role of police undermining

Gates misled Obama with untruths, lies an appeal not defining

Obama being misled erred in support of Gate's delusion

This added to the mistaken conclusion

Crowley the sergeant was too smart to be provoked by baits

He was supported by the black sergeant who identified Gates

Insensitively exposing Obama to disdain and ridicule

Identifies Gates as pitiful, racist and a scourge to his school

A professor of vile, incorrect facts and tainted ideology

Stamps Gates as a dinosaur without a cause or apology

When racists like Gates passes from the scene for all time

Harmonious relations of all people will emerge just fine

The spread of poison from Gate's teaching and writing

Does nothing of note but adds to inciting

Gates would be merciful if he disappeared from the scene

And ceased ruining lives of the young who are innocent and serene

An educator leads, motivates, inspires in positive fashion

Gates infects, poisons, abets hard feelings with passion

Is the Name Obama or Obuma?

Obama sailed to victory with claims of answers and solutions

The excessive wind and oratory he did decry
Collapsed, deflated, metamorphosis into a big lie

The presidential honeymoon is over and done
Not a single victory has the wind won

Exaggerated words, double talk accomplishes nil,
Afghanistan, Iraq, N. Korea, healthcare, economy remains the same ill

The American people by Obama has been had
Cries of Obama, Obama, Obama did resound

Slogans now are Obuma, Obuma, Obuma are you still around?

Fooling people is temporary ground gained when the masses wise up Obama will be pained

Jackson Does it Again

Jesse wanted lenders to make unsafe loans to unqualified black buyers

He is responsible for all the black criers

Many black people now lose their homes in areas under assault

This is Jesse's doing and his fault

Next he turns to Fenger and Marshall the scene of black youngsters in riot

To get his name in print as savior but no one will buy it

He set poor examples for students to follow law and behave

When they kill and riot he pretends to be sympathetic and grave

Jackson the media addict will create the incident with malicious intent

Then appear to pacify, comfort and solace with sincere repent

The cost to black youngsters from this man

Is a police record, jail time and a life with no plan

Black youngsters should follow Obama and Holder for ways to act

They suggest, behave, show tolerance and harmoniously interact

False leaders like Wright, Meeks, Sharpton to name a few

Do grievous harm to minds of children for their names to be in view

Young people can take the path to success in this life's fray

By following the leaders who demonstrate the correct way

Obama Health Care Plan

I need a flu shot to avoid pneumonia and a cold
Was told they ran out but was assured I'm in the fold

I requested a shot for swine flu
Was informed the clouted got it not me or you

Mother needed a liver transplant in urgent situation
They said the alderman put someone ahead of her who was a relation

Next time the waiting was long and took hours nine
Clouted people went ahead of the pack, walked in past the line

Anthology of Poems

Cost to insure 50 million more will not be a cure
This will cause taxes and inflation for sure

The plan is unworkable and will effect stagnation
Infecting the economy with contagion

Obama needs any kind of plan to get through
For re-election he must make a showing it's true

Doctors will work more for less and be ill fated
Health care as we know it will be poorly rated

Foreign VIPs and national leaders will bypass our health program
Because our healthcare will be a sham

Dalward J DeBruzzi

Ode to Self Proclaimed Mr. Clean – Governor Quinn

Quinn served many years with Blago over time

Never saw, heard, or suspected a crime

Quinn says he heard no evil saw no evil but states with elation

He would clean up corruption on his station

He first announced rejection of the tainted Buress's appointment

Drew threat of harm at the polls, from a few black ministers without right or ethic

Pressed his lips to their anal apertures, created a suction of a world class emetic

Next Quinn the mythomanic stated he will restore the image of the University

He proclaimed the head and all the trustees must go to end adversity

Two refused and threats of loss of votes from black ministers brought Quinn pain

Quinn puckered his lips again to his favorite spot and allowed the two, too remain

Quinn ignored the age old pension scam by the "so called public servants", and left it intact

It would have saved the state millions but he did not act

Dalward J DeBruzzi

Quinn huffed and puffed about cost cutting with a bang

But took no steps to eliminate automatic raises for the political gang

Quinn's false claims for election rules improvement, was forlorn

He made no advances in election reform

Quinn failed to limit legislator's years of range

Another failure and exposure of his failure to make change

Quinn claims, doubling he income tax is good for you and me

This is probably the only thing he will get passed you see

Quinn's only cost cutting to save money aside

Will be to take away elderly citizen's ride

Quinn lacks a spine, has strong lips, no worthy programs of any kind
Citizens will reject him, his graft and ideas

and defeat him with a firm mind

Parents

My father and mother worked for a family to support
They worked long hours, duties they did not abort

They did without things many times over
Provided us kids with goodies, we were in clover

Our clothes were nice, modest, warm, and oh so neat
They ceaselessly toiled for us, never skipped a beat

They sometimes worked at jobs better not to mention
They sacrificed, labored, with consistent convention

College was costly, but my parents came through
With books, board, tuition it was ever so true

Now us kids are married with kids of our own
Our parents are slow'n up, old they have grown

Their uselessness to us is a description of gloom
To inherit it all, we hope they're ready for a tomb

INGRATITUDE

Persistence

Working as a stock boy wasn't an allure
Boring, low pay, it wasn't for me for sure

Fixing cars was tough, dirty, held no attraction for me
Challenging, profitable, demanding but with me did not agree

Consulted professional employment agency to assess my qualifications
Errand boy, messenger, floor scrubber caused no excited palpitations

Faced facts, went back to school for years
Emerged a professional, glorious, happy, with joyful tears

When seeking and striving to find one's way
Frustration, grief, sobs make it easy to stray

Persevering, sticking to established goals
Dismisses failures, impediments, denies obstructing shoals

        SUCCESS

Scorn Can Be Fatal

Custer and the Seventh Cavalry rode upright and proud
Banners flying, horses prancing, band playing Loud

Unwisely split his command in troops three small
Thinking scornfully, savages no ability at all

Felt the primitives would tremble, disperse and run
Order sabers drawn and begin his fun

Failed to see that when fighting for life
Gives purpose and heart to combat strife

Sitting Bull and Crazy Horse too, knew his yen for killing its true
Instilled vengeful hearts, meant to follow through

Savages assembled an army of brave men
To deliver a blow of surprise to Custer then

When fully ringed with massed men who were brave
Custer sensed his errors, felt there would be no save

Custer believed in his own might and great feat
Suffered a disastrous, bloody, loss and was fatally beat

Never scorn and denigrate an enemy of will
It may prove, deadly, render you fatally from the kill

The only gain for Custer from all that you can bet
Is by dying there, he is remembered yet

Dalward J DeBruzzi

Seeking the One

When we are lost and wandering and seeking
    for each other
We seek and look intently
Our goal dismisses bother

The good and faithful seeker
Is relentless in his mission
Proclaims aloud as speaker
Pleading his quest to listen

Our glorious hearts say, soon we'll weld
Into one common heartbeat
To each as we are held
We become salvation, a mutual treat

HAPPINESS

Serving Who?

If I become a politician it would be unreal
But how wonderful, a license to steal

Gosh, wow, I got elected
It's great they believed me and I got selected

George Ryan, Blago, dozens of alderman all
    grabbed, stole and ran
The same with me, I will load up and pilfer
    all I can

Today five kids to special schools I clouted
Even though they didn't deserve it and the
    people shouted

Serve who? I got my family and relatives
    even though, unqualified, jobs
Despite some were loafers, dumb, lazy and
    slobs

Elected to serve! Yes but I'm serving me, and stealing and causing a lot of grief
But unlike most I am honest and admit, I'm just a thief

POLITICIAN

Thankfulness!

Join me in the morning hours
Ere problems, snags cause sorrows

People awake from nightly rest
Look to a day that's yet the best

Join me in midday hours
Good people, goodness and lovely flowers

Join me in the twilight hours
Satisfaction, appreciation, peace, soft evening
    showers

A WONDERFUL DAY!

Dalward J DeBruzzi

The Indian's Fate

Indians were our earliest human creatures here
Helpful kind, greeting us with good cheer

Pushed out of the Eastern seaboard states
Left wanting with little left on their plates

To save their land and be crowded no more
Signed treaties, broken when they walked out the door

Trading whiskey, trinkets and cheating big time
Indians greatly suffered and it was a crime

Buffaloes provided clothes, robes and food
They were killed off and thus created a feud

Rather than starve and beg, they raided to live
For Indian agents had food, blankets but didn't give

Told to farm and raise crops for their meals
The land given were rocks and poor fields

Indians now laugh at us heartily all day
They own Casinos and make a lot of hay

Getting back at us for all their bad deals
They gleefully grab our money and enjoy our squeals

Thinking Big

I dream of riches, fortunes and gold
Wishes, thoughts yearnings of old

My taste for yachts, fine cars and limousines
Quenching appetites with exquisite cuisines

Mansions, fine clothes and real estate
Are things that I highly value and appreciate

In the library my scale of values changed for sure
She was bespectacled, pert, refreshing, different and demure

Altered goals now included home, children and wife
Riches, materiality now unnecessary for the content life

Thinking big is people, love and living
Satisfaction is found in the secret of mutual giving

What I Say Sounds Good
You Can Quote Me Barack Obama

When I ran against Bush the incumbent
I said unemployment was his fault
Now its worse and I must repent

I said Bush didn't know how to handle Korea
To get rid of their nukes
Now that I've failed I get diarrhea

I said Bush didn't know how to approach Iran
To discourage their trend
My magic promise failed for I had no plan

My friend Henry Gates broke the law its clear
To create an incident
I covered the embarrassment with a beer

Farrakan, Meeks and Wright, my spiritual guides
Are racist and venomous
They are offensive, militant and take sides

Rezko my former mentor is now in federal jail
For crimes numerous
My disassociation will hopefully prevail

For 20 years in a Trinity pew I sat hearing
Wright hating Jews, Whites and the country
Never once did I hear that
Maybe it's because of where I sat

Not hearing Wright's poison spears
At anytime
Can be explained by malfunctioning ears

Wife Michelle was proud of U.S.A only once
In her life
For a first lady to admit makes her a dunce

Our relations abroad are no better
Than with Bush
In a speech I will make it sound like a love letter

I deliver a speech with hope and change
To pep everyone up
But with no improvement it sounds strange

If music was bull shit in this land
And nothing more
I could be a one man symphonic band

Why Illinois is 13 Billion in Debt

Governor Ryan took payoffs, bribes, and the taxpayers for everything they got
Swore, cried, denied and pleaded innocent till the last and said he did not

While he stole from the public and plundered
The state legislature never wondered

Blagoiavitch came in, took even more and more
Took everything and cleaned out the store

The legislature saw nothing amiss in the thievery and stealing
If you're getting yours why start squealing?

Blagoiavitch was indicted and accused of dishonest persuasion
He robbed and raided on every occasion

While Blago stole without restraint and fairness
The legislature looked away and pretended unawareness

Quinn steps in claiming to be Mr. Clean and not a party to anything of evil note
He failed to unseat the tainted Burris when threatened by loss of vote

He pledged to restore the U. of Illinois' reputation with changes of appointment
Two refused to resign and he again caved in to Black ministers' threats to refuse anointment

The legislature looked far and away and said not a word
Cause they cheated the rightful students and animosity occurred

Dalward J DeBruzzi

With three governors and the same legislature
    we still have pension abuse
Who is the cause of public's criminal use?

The latest team of Quinn and the legislature
    of the State
Indicates the continuing public rape to date

With Fondest Childhood Memories

When I was just a little tot
It dawned on me, became aware

How God loves all his children
Keeping them tenderly in his care

I recall home so well with love not dread
Snug in my soft, warm cozy, bed

I remember details of childhood days
Clearly in my heart, easily as one sees
Visions of sweetest memories

We thank you deeply God
For food, drink and bread
You also provided things I read

I remember my childhood years
With parental labor, love and protection
Thanks, gratitude, and my folks for election

Dalward J DeBruzzi

Golden thoughts of childhood
Are lovingly, fondly rethought
The nostalgic memories are something that can't be bought

Youth

Youth is young, handsome healthy,
unafraid and knows not why

Inexperience, ignorance, enthusiasm,
ambition allows all things to try

No hesitance, no doubts, no flinching at
all, with feelings that life has no fall

Youth conquers, youth wins, youth exudes
confidence, life will be a ball

Disappointments start to occur, failures
begin to appear

Seepage creeps in and growth of vestiges
of trauma, loom like fear

Dalward J DeBruzzi

Gradual comprehension of individual limitations do cause despair

This in addition to the startling development, some loss of hair

Not reaching goals and ambitions, bring disheartening broods

Maturity insulates, reinforces courage, and values to weather down moods

Twilights of life reflects past saga of passage through time

Old age remains content, satisfying, undaunted but in rhyme

Maximum undying effort on every attempt
in the struggle of life

In final repose no regrets no tragic reviews,
all was exerted without escape from strife

Youth is wonderful, temporary, vibrant,
wholesome and should not be wasted

Caution when expending your youth
It never comes back and that's the truth

CPSIA information can be obtained at www.ICGtesting.com
Printed in the USA
LVOW10s1108240415

435957LV00018B/172/P